R. H. Dunn

18 th September 2000

BRANCH LINES AROUND MARCH

from Ely, St. Ives, Ramsey, Peterborough, Murrow and Wisbech

Vic Mitchell Keith Smith
Christopher Awdry and Allan Mott

Cover picture: Class J20 no. 64683 struggles with a heavy freight from Whitemoor Yard on 3rd April 1956. The train is on the line that avoided the four through platforms at March. (P.Hay)

First Published February 1993
Reprinted November 1998

ISBN 1 873793 09 X

© *Middleton Press, 1993*

Design Deborah Goodridge

Published by
    Middleton Press
    Easebourne Lane
    Midhurst, West Sussex
    GU29 9AZ
Tel: 01730 813169
Fax: 01730 812601

Printed & bound by Biddles Ltd,
    Guildford and Kings Lynn

CONTENTS

ACKNOWLEDGEMENTS

In addition to those people mentioned in the text, the authors are grateful for the help, during the preparation of this this book, of D.Brown, R.Butt, G.Croughton, J.Ellis, A.J.Fall, A.G.W.Garraway, C.Grimwood, Miss L.S.James, H.N.James, A.E.Mansfield, R.I.Burn-Murdoch, C.Palmer, C.Parkinson, D.Salter, P.C.Saunders, N.Stanyon, Prof. H.P.White, L.Wright, P.Wright, E.S.Youldon the staff of Cambridge University Library and our wives.

INDEX

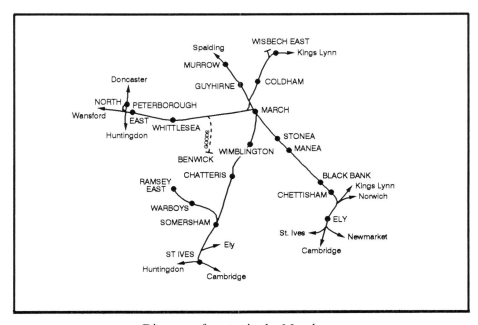

Diagram of routes in the March area.

GEOGRAPHICAL SETTING

March lies at the centre of a rich agricultural area, in the heart of the Cambridgeshire Fens. Agricultural produce therefore played a very important role in the economy of the area and accounted for the provision of goods facilities which would appear lavish in many other places. The land is flat for the most part, and the steepest gradients found on any of these lines are usually those required to raise them across the many drains and dykes which vein the district. Continual watch has to be kept on the trackbeds, as the peat beneath them dries and shrinks, affecting the levels.

All the maps are to the scale of 25" to 1 mile, unless otherwise shown, and all are from the 1901-03 edition.

1930 map at 4 miles to 1 inch.

HISTORICAL BACKGROUND

The first station opened in the area at Ely on 29th July 1845, when the Eastern Counties Railway extended the original Northern & Eastern Railway's route to Brandon via Cambridge. The branch through March to Peterborough was being built at the same time, and was opened for general traffic on 14th January 1847. The Wisbech, St Ives & Cambridge Junction Railway opened to a station at the present site of Wisbech Goods on 3rd May 1847. The ECR came into conflict with the Lynn & Ely Railway at this point. The L&ER had built a branch to Wisbech from Watlington, on its main line, opening its own station at right angles to the earlier one on 2nd February 1848. After an agreement with the Great Northern Railway, it planned to run trains to Peterborough via a linking curve and the ECR. The ECR (which owned the curve) is reputed to have countered this not unreasonable desire by fixing sleepers across the line on the curve, and the upshot of a lengthy dispute was that the ECR took over the operation of the L&ER from 1st January 1852. It may be assumed that the original ECR station closed for passengers at that time.

The line from March to St Ives was also authorised to the Wisbech, St Ives & Cambridge Junction Railway (though the ECR had a large hand in building it), and opened on 1st February 1848 for goods, a month later for passengers.

The final leg of our Fenland "spider" was the line which later became the GN/GE Joint one, but began as a branch south to March from Spalding, built by the Great Northern Railway. It was therefore the GNR which provided the original sidings that became the nucleus of the later Whitemoor Yard. This line opened on 1st April 1867, almost five years after the ECR had become the major part of the new Great Eastern Railway. The GER quickly saw that the GN line could offer access to the coalfields of Yorkshire, thus acquiring not only cheaper fuel for itself, but some steady business with housecoal into the bargain. After some years of agitation and an incredible amount of wrangling, a joint GN & GE Committee was formed on 3rd July 1879. It was to build a new line from Spalding to Lincoln, and in addition to take over existing lines between Lincoln and Black Carr Junction, (on the GNR south of Doncaster), Spalding and Grassmoor Junction, (north of March), March and Needingworth Junction, (a little north of St Ives), and St.Ives to Huntingdon. The branch between Somersham and Ramsey was opened on 16th September 1889.

All the lines covered in this volume, other than the joint ones just mentioned, became GER property when that company was formed on 7 August 1862. All, without exception, came to the London & North Eastern Railway at the Grouping in 1923. Closures took place as follows -

	GOODS	PASSENGER
Somersham - Ramsey East	17 Sept 1956	22 Sept 1930
March - St. Ives	18 April 1966	6 March 1967
March - Wisbech	-	9 Sept 1968
March - Spalding	5 October 1964	15 May 1983

PASSENGER SERVICES

Spalding to March

Services on the line were fairly sparse, the June 1869 timetable showing just three weekday trains each way, plus a rather curious Tuesdays only service which left Spalding at 7.00am and ran as far as Murrow, returning from there at 7.45am. There was never a Sunday service to Murrow or Guyhirne. After the line became part of the Joint route, a thrice daily service between Liverpool Street and Doncaster via Cambridge was run from 1st August 1882. The local service in 1890 had increased to five trains a day, and by the beginning of World War I trains were running through to York, and the harbinger of the Harwich/North West boat trains had begun by then too. In 1938 there was a local service of six trains. The boat trains were taken off at the beginning of WWII but were reintroduced from Colchester to Manchester and York for the benefit of service personnel. They were extended to Harwich when troopships started running regularly. By 1946 the local stoppers

1. Peterborough North was the city's main station, but it was not the first. It opened only in 1850, with the arrival of the Great Northern Railway's line from London. This view, taken on 9th September 1958, looks north and shows the overall roof across the main line on the right. Birmingham and March trains used the left-hand face of the island platform, with the avoiding line to the west of that. Further left, beyond the row of signal-wire guideposts, lie the ex-Midland Railway tracks, with that company's yard on the extreme left. The Midland engine shed here closed on 31st January 1960. (H.P.White)

2. The facade of Peterborough North station is seen during the summer of 1958. The low tower with the hipped roof was at the eastern end of the footbridge, goods facilities were at the near end of the facade, with station offices at the other. The writer recalls an aroma of mailbags which seemed to hang perennially over the station, except when the wind was from the north. Whipping through the windtunnel of the roofed area, this wind drove everything, mailbag smells included, mercilessly before it. (H.P.White)

3. The suffix "North" was dropped in 1966 when East station was closed. This picture, taken during the summer of 1990, shows remodelled trackwork and a rebuilt station. Up trains use the through platform to the right, and the fast through lines run to the left of the central platform. A new island platform on the left caters for down traffic from London and trains taking the cross-country lines. The ex-MR yard still has track into it, but the coaling tower has gone. The only real landmarks remaining from the 1958 picture are the Great Northern Hotel, on the right, and the office block in the left distance. The hotel was one of many once owned by the GNR. (A.Mott)

4. By 1989 the facade had undergone a complete transformation, the only thing remaining roughly the same being the site of the entrance and the general road layout. Due to its deteriorating condition, the station was rebuilt and officially reopened by Sir Peter Parker on 30th September 1980. (A.Mott)

5. Crescent Bridge is south of the station and is seen in 1991. The long bow-string girder bridge was completed in 1913 to remove what was becoming, even then, a notorious level-crossing. The site of the MR's Crescent station was on the left. (A.Mott)

6. A view south from Crescent Bridge in 1969 includes a rake of fly-ash hoppers on the right (west), beside the line leading down to the River Nene bridge, used by trains heading to March. The down through line cuts diagonally across the picture, and the Nene carriage sidings lie in the centre. Peterborough power station, now demolished, dominates the line to London, which curves on to the Nene viaduct. (A.Mott)

July 1915

ELY, MARCH, and PETERBRO'.—Great Eastern.

Down. — Week Days.

Miles from Ely.	Down.	mrn	mrn	mrn	mrn	mrn	mrn	aft	mrn	mrn	aft	aft	aft	aft	aft	aft	aft	aft	aft	aft
	310 Cambridge ....dep.	....	8 12	8 20	....	1017	1055	....	1158	....	1233	1 24	1 31	4 12	5 20	6 12	....	7 25	8 30	1150
	325 Harwich (Town). "	....	....	....	....	....	Via St. Ives.	....	1014	....	....	....	Via St. Ives.	12 19	....	3 38	....	....	4 31	....
	314 " (P. Q.).. "	....	....	....	....	....		....	1022	....	....	....		12 27	....	3 46	....	....	4 39	....
	312 Yarmouth (Vaux.) "	....	....	....	....	8 17		....	10 1	1032	....	....		12 55	2 20	4 12	....	....	Via St. Ives.	9 15
	312 Lowestoft (Cen.). "	....	....	....	....	7 30		Saturdays only.	9 46	....	....	....		12 40	....	4 2	....	....		9 0
	316 Cromer .... "	....	....	....	....	8 3			9 20	....	....	....		12 55	2 29	3 38	....	....		9 7
	312 Norwich (Thorpe) "	....	....	....	....	9 8			1047	1120	....	....		1 57	3 33	4 57	....	....		1024
—	Ely ....dep.	....	8 55	....	....	1046			1233	....	1 1	1 55		4 49	5 59	6 36	6 42	7 51		1230
3¼	Chettisham	....	9 2	....	....	1053			....	....	....	2 2		4 56	....	....	6 49	....		ngt.
5	Black Bank†	....	9 6	....	....	1057			....	....	....	2 6		5 0	....	....	6 53	....		....
9¾	Manea	....	9 15	....	....	11 6			....	....	1n15	2 15		5 9	....	....	7 2	....		....
11½	Stonea	....	9 20	....	....	1111			....	....	....	2 20		5 14	....	....	7 7	....		....
15¼	March 315, 321, 358 arr.	....	9 26	9 29	....	1117	12 3		1254	1 4	1 22	2 26	2 39	5 20	6 20	6 57	7 13	8 12	9 39	1257
	dep.	8 15	9 40		1058	1120	....	1210	1 15		1 30	3 4		5 32	....	7 5	7 20	8 25	9 42	1 3
24¼	Whittlesea	8 27	9 52		1110	1132	....	1222	....		....	3 16		5 44	....	....	7 32	8 39	9 54	1 18
29¼	Peterbro' (G. E.) 470, 643 arr.	8 38	10 4		1122	1144	....	1234	1 38		1 50	3 27		5 56	....	7 25	7 44	8 50	10 5	1 43
	dep.	....	10 8		1124	1158	....	....	....		1 55	3 36		6 2	....	....	7 50	....	....	1 50
30¼	" (G. N.) 366. arr.	....	1012		1128	12 4	....	....	....		1 59	3 40		6 5	....	....	7 53	....	....	1 55

Down. — Sundays.

Miles from Ely.	Down.	mrn	mrn	aft	aft	aft
	310 Cambridge ....dep.	....	1124	5 0	5 15	1135
	325 Harwich (Town). "	6 50	8g40	9g0	Via St. Ives.	6b7
	314 " (P. Q.).. "	7 0	8g48	9g8		6b14
	312 Yarmouth (Vaux.) "	....	....	1 20		9 15
	312 Lowestoft (Cen.). "	....	....	1 12		9 0
	316 Cromer .... "	....	....	1 0		8 0
	312 Norwich (Thorpe) "	....	....	2 29		1024
—	Ely ....dep.	9 10	1148	5 4[illegible]		1230
3¼	Chettisham	....	....	Sig.		ngt.
5	Black Bank†	....	....	Sig.		....
9¾	Manea	....	....	6 7		....
11½	Stonea	....	....	Sig.		....
15¼	March 315, 321, 358 arr.	9 31	1210	6 20	6 25	1257
	dep.	9 35	....	6 28	6 28	1 3
24¼	Whittlesea	....	....	6 40	6 40	1 18
29¼	Peterbro' (G. E.) 470, 643 arr.	9 55	....	6 52	6 52	1 43
	dep.	....	....	....	....	1 50
30¼	" (G. N.) 366. arr.	....	....	....	....	1 55

Up. — Week Days.

Miles.	Up.	mrn	mrn	mrn	mrn	mrn	mrn	mrn	aft	aft	aft	aft	aft	aft	aft	aft	aft	aft	aft
	Peterbro' (G.N.)......dep.	....	6 45	....	9 17	....	....	....	....	1235	2 22	....	....	....		4 23	6 35	....	....
	" (G.E.).... arr.	....	6 50	....	9 20	....	....	....	....	1240	2 27	....	....	....		4 28	6 40	....	....
—	dep.	6 24	7 8	7 8	9 26	9 50	....	1036	1238	1 0	2 33	....	....	3 35		5 3	7 0	....	1058
5¼	Whittlesea	6 34	7 18	7 18	9 36	10 0	....	1046	1248	....	2 43	....	....	3 45		5 13	7 10	....	1110
14	March 315, 321, 358 arr.	6 46	7 30	7 30	9 48	1012	....	1058	1 2	1 20	2 55	....	....	3 55		5 25	7 22	....	1126
	dep.	6 50	7 37	8 9	9 54	1019	1027	....	1 9	1 25	3 14	3 34	3 51	4 8	5 31	5 37	8 10	8 24	1134
18	Stonea	6 57	Via St. Ives.	....	10 1	....	Via St. Ives.	....	1 16	....	Via St. Ives.	3 41	....	....	Via St. Ives.	5 44	....	Via St. Ives.	a
19¾	Manea	7 2		....	10 6	....		....	1 21	....		3 46	....	....		5 49	....		r
24¼	Black Bank†	7 11		....	10 15	....		....	1 30	....		3 55	....	....		5 58	....		....
26¼	Chettisham ....[318, 321	7 15		....	10 19	....		....	1 34	....		3 59	....	....		6 2	....		....
29½	Ely 310, 312, 314, arr.	7 21		8 30	10 25	1040		....	1 40	1 46		4 5	4 12	4 29		6 8	8 31		1158
83¼	310 Norwich (Thorpe) arr.	....		10 30	12 0	....		....	3 28	3 28		....	5 50	6 9		9 32	10 6		2 0
107¼	316 Cromer .... "	....		12 1	2 10	....		....	4 56	4 56		....	....	7 38		1033	....		....
106¼	310 Lowestoft (Cen.). "	....		12 25	2 23	....		....	4 37	4 37		....	6 51	7 5		1045	....		....
100¾	310 Yarmouth (Vaux.) "	....		12 8	12 59	....		....	4 39	4 39		....	6 45	7 5		1031	10 59		3 0
102¾	314 Harwich (P. Q.).. "	....		1 58	2 21	2 21		....	....	....		....	6 53	6 53		1053	11k56		....
104¼	325 " (Town).. "	....		2 5	2 28	2 28		....	....	....		....	7 0	7 0		11 0	12k3		....
44¼	312 Cambridge .... "	7 46	8 50	9 0	11 9	11 9	1138	....	2 14	2 14	4 25	....	4 37	5 9	6 45	6 54	8 59	9 34	1245

Up. — Sundays.

Miles.	Up.	aft	aft	aft	aft
	Peterbro' (G.N.)......dep.	....	....	....	10 0
	" (G.E.).... arr.	....	....	....	10 5
—	dep.	3 8	....	4 40	1058
5¼	Whittlesea	3 18	....	....	1110
14	March 315, 321, 358 arr.	3 30	....	5 0	1126
	dep.	3 40	4 55	5 3	1134
18	Stonea	3 48	....	....	....
19¾	Manea	3 53	....	....	....
24¼	Black Bank†	4 2	....	....	....
26¼	Chettisham ....[318, 321	4 6	....	....	....
29½	Ely 310, 312, 314, arr.	4 13	5 15	5 24	1158
83¼	310 Norwich (Thorpe) arr.	....	....	7 29	2 0
107¼	316 Cromer .... "	....	....	10 5	....
106¼	310 Lowestoft (Cen.). "	....	....	8 37	....
100¾	310 Yarmouth (Vaux.) "	....	....	8 31	3 0
102¾	314 Harwich (P. Q.).. "	....	....	9 31	....
104¼	325 " (Town).. "	....	....	9 38	....
44¼	312 Cambridge .... "	5 0	5 42	8 11	1245

a Stops on Saturdays at 11 41 aft. when required to set down.

b Via Sudbury and Cambridge.

g Via Cambridge.

k Wednesdays and Saturdays.

n Wednesdays only.

r Stops on Saturdays at 11 46 aft. when required to set down.

† Station for Downham Village.

7. Super-Sprinter no.158764 crosses the River Nene on 5th March 1992 and heads up towards Peterborough station. It formed the 1308 to Liverpool, on this occasion running a little late. The ex-GN Nene viaduct stands in the background, the Sprinter having just crossed beneath the span seen directly behind the the second and third carriages. The end of the privately operated Nene Valley Railway is on the right. (A.Mott)

8. The same span again but on 25th May 1991 and seen this time from the site of the Nene Valley Railway's Peterborough station. The locomotive is a Polish Kreigslok 2-10-0, acquired in 1990. Closer to the bridge, on the left, stands a Matheron locomotive from Bombay - both engines are ultimately intended as Railworld exhibits at a project planned for establishment in this area. (A.Mott)

L. N. E. R.
FURLOUGH
FOR CONDITIONS SEE BACK
Available for three days including day of issue
PETERBORO EAST to
WHITTLESEA
THIRD / Fur. 3in. \ CLASS
1279
WHITTLESEA
5126   5126

9. Here the bridge is viewed from the other (eastern) side, in 1969. The line to the former North station snakes off to the right, while the connection towards Wansford was still in place to serve the local sugar-beet factory. The passenger service to Rugby via Market Harborough had ceased on 6th June 1966, and to Northampton via Wellingborough even earlier, on 4th May 1964. (A.Mott)

PETERBOROUGH EAST

10. The facade of Peterborough East station; few changes had taken place between its opening and the date of this picture, 1972, taken just prior to demolition. It was a handsome building, sometimes attributed to J R. Livock, but more in the style of Sancton Wood, architect for both the ECR and the Syston & Peterborough Railway. (A.V.Fincham)

12. A Stanier 8F 2-8-0 no.48061 heads a Class 5 freight out of Peterborough East yard in about 1958, no doubt heading back towards its home base at Leicester Midland (15C). (H.Cooke)

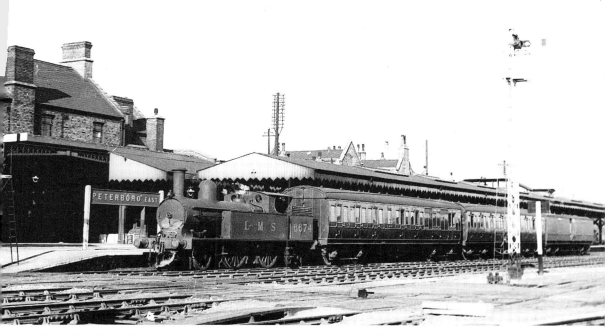

11. It is 20th May 1938, and an ex-London & North Western 2-4-2 radial tank stands with a local train, probably destined for Northampton. Classified 1P by the LMS, no.6674 was one of a class designed by F.W.Webb, and built between 1890 and 1897. This example had been withdrawn by the Nationalisation of 1948, and the rest had gone by 1955. The first vehicle in the non-corridor train is a timber 3rd brake composite of a type designed by R.W.Reid for the LMS and introduced from 1933. The second carriage is a slightly later steel-sided all 3rd, and the last vehicle is a postal van. Note the abbreviated station nameboard. (H.C.Casserley)

13. The signalbox on stilts was an unusual feature, and with a main running line below must have been somewhat unsettling for signalmen until they got used to it. It survived the station's closure to passengers on 6th June 1966 by some years, since goods facilities continued, but was finally demolished, along with the station, in 1972. The goods arrangements can be seen on the right of this 1969 picture, as a DMU from Cambridge passes by. (A.Mott)

14. This picture is taken from the same viewpoint on 5th March 1992. A pair of Class 31s heads east on plain track towards the viaduct which now carries Peterborough's ringroad. In the left middle distance is the old goods shed, now in commercial use, and beyond it is the six-road engine shed.   In August 1992, this building received a Grade II listing from the Department of National Heritage. (A.Mott)

KINGS DYKE

15. Class D16/3 4-4-0 no.62548 hurries past Kings Dyke brickworks with a semi-fast from Peterborough in April 1956. These engines were widely used on passenger services in the Fens during the 1950s, but within four years of this picture only one - 62613 - survived. The train is a mixture of Gresley and Thompson LNER stock. (P.Hay)

Kings Dyke, some three miles east of Peterborough East, retains its level crossing, and the map shows branches, now severed, into the brickworks. The London Brick Company was one of the larger employers in the district, with no fewer than three brickworks - Itter, Central and Saxon - between Peterborough and Whittlesea. Itter became known as Kings Dyke after a nearby watercourse.

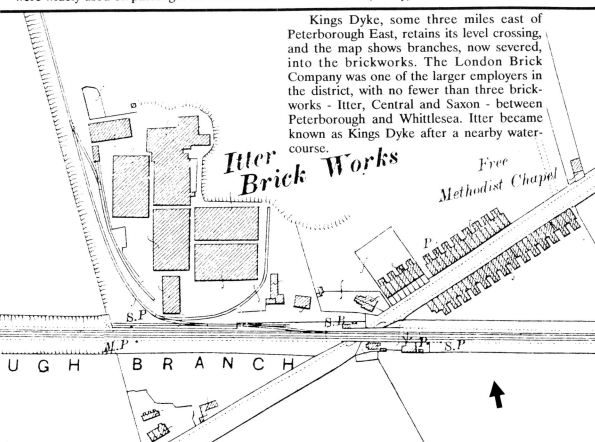

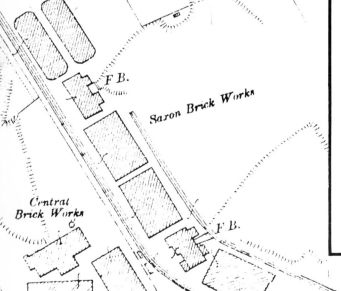

Central and Saxon Brickworks were east of Itter Works.

16. This picture is taken at the same place on the same day, but looks east rather than west. Holden Class J17 0-6-0 no.65583 trundles towards Whittlesea with a freight, past Saxon (nearer) and Central brickyards. (P.Hay)

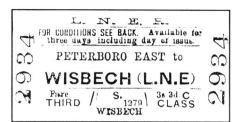

17. Kings Dyke signalbox guards the level crossing of the railway with the A605 Peterborough/Whittlesey road, and was still very much in business in 1992. The barriers are down on a day in 1989, though the further one looks a trifle bent. (A.Mott)

WHITTLESEA

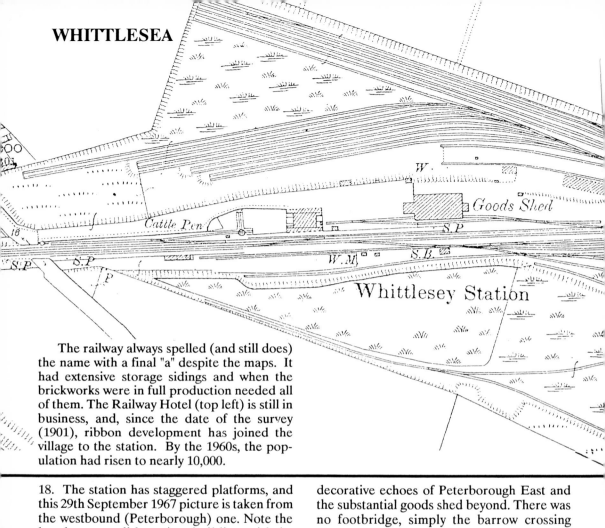

The railway always spelled (and still does) the name with a final "a" despite the maps. It had extensive storage sidings and when the brickworks were in full production needed all of them. The Railway Hotel (top left) is still in business, and, since the date of the survey (1901), ribbon development has joined the village to the station. By the 1960s, the population had risen to nearly 10,000.

18. The station has staggered platforms, and this 29th September 1967 picture is taken from the westbound (Peterborough) one. Note the handsome, solid station building with its decorative echoes of Peterborough East and the substantial goods shed beyond. There was no footbridge, simply the barrow crossing shown. (R.M.Casserley)

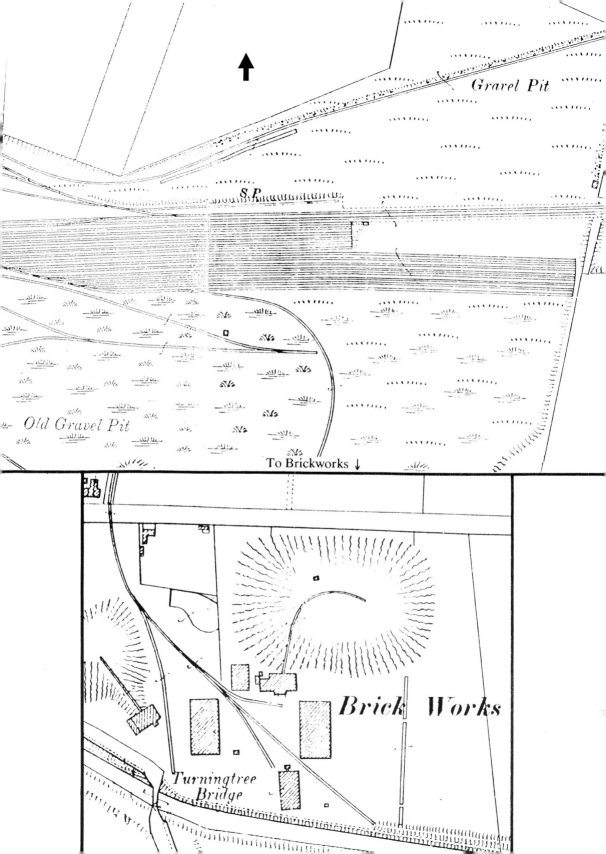

Gravel Pit

S.P.

Old Gravel Pit

To Brickworks ↓

Brick Works

Turningtree
Bridge

19. Class B1 4-6-0 no.61391 pauses at Whittlesea with the Railway Correspondence & Travel Society "Fensman" tour on 9th September 1956. We shall meet this tour again at Benwick, and it also visited the Wisbech & Upwell Tramway on the same day. Note the notched signal arms still extant in both directions. (E.Sawford)

20. These are the facilities available in 1992, shown in a picture dated 12th October 1989. No more than necessary, perhaps, but a comedown from picture 18, and an awfully long walk to the Cambridge platform shelter if it happens to be raining. (A.Mott)

21. The level crossing at Whittlesea is a busy one, the man in the previously-shown hut combining duties as booking clerk with those of crossing keeper. Traffic waits at the crossing on 4th April 1988, queueing back past the Railway Inn and the carriage it keeps as a restaurant. (A.Mott)

22. Sprinter no.156440, bound for Norwich on 9th January 1992, heads towards Ely past a smart-looking signalbox. The siding on the left, once serving a factory, was closed in 1989 and has now been cannibalised by the pw gang for spares. It is tempting to wonder how long it might be before an electric link between Ely and Peterborough is made. (A.Mott)

THREE HORSE SHOES JUNCTION

23. Three Horse Shoes signalbox was named after a local hostelry, and here we see it in February 1992. It commanded the entrance to the Benwick branch, and is a solid brick affair, but one cannot imagine its signalman's duties as ever being arduous, even when both the branch and the siding situated nearby were in operation. (A.Mott)

From Three Horse Shoes Junction a single track curved sharply to the south, going more or less straight to Benwick, where there was a final curve towards the west. Built under a Light Railway Order and opened throughout on 2nd August 1898, it was never more than a goods line. During World War II, Benwick depot was disguised as Whitemoor to deceive the Luftwaffe, but does not appear to have attracted much extra attention as a result.

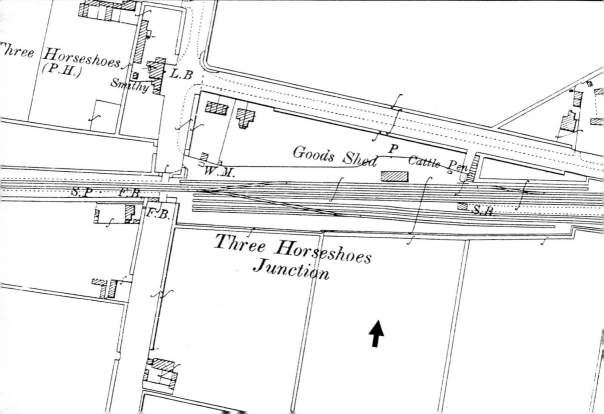

BENWICK BRANCH

1906 map at 1" to 1 mile, showing the entire branch.

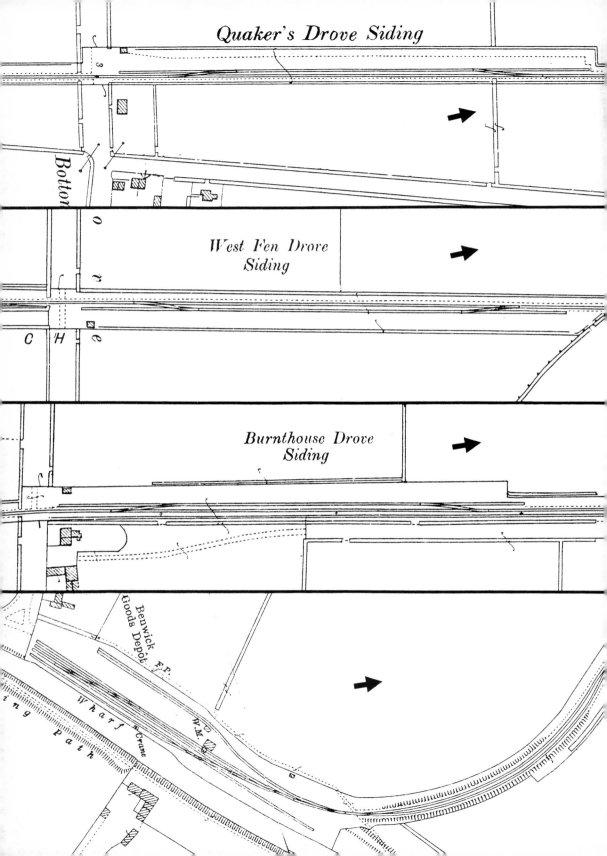

Quaker's Drove Siding

West Fen Drove
Siding

Burnthouse Drove
Siding

Benwick F.P.
Goods Depôt

24. This print of the goods depot at Benwick is undated, but the style of the road transport would seem to suggest c1940. The low angle of the picture emphasises the featurelessness (mistaken by many for dullness) of the fenland landscape. (D.Thompson)

25. The RCTS tour on 9th September 1956 approaches Benwick behind Class J17 0-6-0 no.65562. Members have forsaken their carriages for open wagons, and later in the day were to get very wet in similar accommodation on the Wisbech & Upwell Tramway. (A.E.Bennett)

26. The line closed on 13th July 1964, but the site of Benwick depot went into commercial use. This shot shows the same entrance as picture 24, but in October 1991, 27 years after the railway left. The address, it is worth noting, is still however, "The Old Station Yard". (A.Mott)

2. Ely towards March
ELY

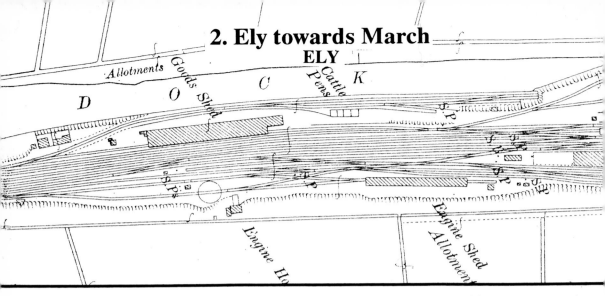

Ely station was built a little way from the centre of the town, south of a loop in the River Ouse. It was an important junction, and with the development of regional express services in the last few years has become even more so, governing lines to Cambridge, St. Ives, March, King's Lynn, Norwich and Bury St. Edmunds. The only casualty has been the St Ives line, so it retains much of this importance today. The line from Cambridge is on the left.

27. The design of Ely station is attributed to Sancton Wood, who was the Eastern Counties Railway architect at the time of the opening of the station on 30th July 1845. (Illustrated London News)

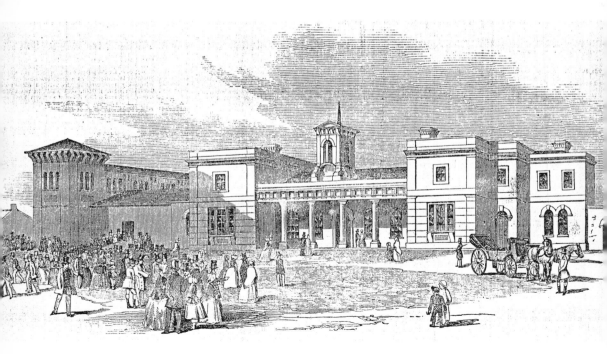

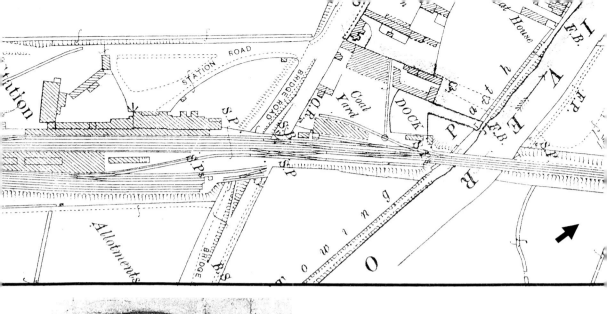

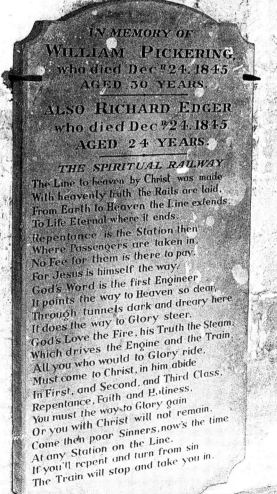

IN MEMORY OF
WILLIAM PICKERING
who died Dec.R 24. 1845
AGED 30 YEARS

ALSO RICHARD EDGER
who died Dec.R 24. 1845
AGED 24 YEARS.

THE SPIRITUAL RAILWAY

The Line to heaven by Christ was made
With heavenly truth the Rails are laid.
From Earth to Heaven the Line extends,
To Life Eternal where it ends.
Repentance is the Station then
Where Passengers are taken in,
No Fee for them is there to pay,
For Jesus is himself the way.
God's Word is the first Engineer
It points the way to Heaven so clear,
Through tunnels dark and dreary here
It does the way to Glory steer.
God's Love the Fire, his Truth the Steam,
Which drives the Engine and the Train,
All you who would to Glory ride,
Must come to Christ, in him abide
In First, and Second, and Third Class,
Repentance, Faith and Holiness,
You must the way to Glory gain
Or you with Christ will not remain.
Come then poor Sinners, now's the time
At any Station on the Line.
If you'll repent and turn from sin
The Train will stop and take you in.

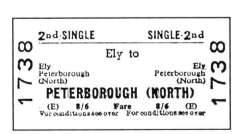

28. Ely Cathedral is the home of one of our
more notable railway memorials. (A.Mott)

29. Shunting at Ely, on 19th September 1953, a two-van rake waits at the down platform before setting back. There is interest in the architecture of the up platform - gaslamps, old-fashioned PA system, and canopy-supports. To judge by the number of people in attendance, a train seems imminent. (H.C.Casserley)

30. Class J17 0-6-0 no.65562 heads a train of tankers past Ely South signalbox on 2nd April 1956. Note part of an articulated set, liveried in "blood and custard", stabled in the background. (P Hay)

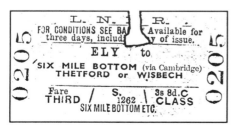

31. Class D16 4-4-0, no. 62553, leaves with a stopping train of Thompson non-corridor stock bound for March. It makes a non-environmentally conscious exit from Ely's down platform during April 1956. (P.Hay)

32. Another D16 4-4-0, no.62558 passes the distant cathedral in 1956. Introduced in 1906, this locomotive had by now been modernised several times, and was destined to be cut up in the following year. The leading coach of the train, with long grab-handles, is ex-Great Eastern as well as the engine. (P.Hay)

33. "Britannia" Class 4-6-2 no.70008 *Black Prince* stands at Ely with an up express, possibly from Norwich, at which place (32A) 70008 was shedded at the time. (S.R.Payne)

GREAT EASTERN RAILWAY
Issued subject to Regulations in the
Company's Time Tables.
MANEA to
Manea   Manea
CHATTERIS
Chatteris   Chatteris
1s. 2d.   FARE   1s. 2d.
Third Class

2429

34. Ivatt Mogul 2-6-0 no.46465 was no stranger at Ely's down platform on 11th March 1961, being at that time shedded at Cambridge (31A). (R.M.Casserley)

35. We look north from the level crossing in 1969 as a southbound DMU crosses towards the up platform. The girders behind the train form the south bridge over the River Ouse. (A.Mott)

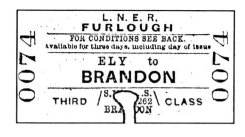

37. This picture was taken in May 1988, and it is comforting to know that the facade will survive. (A Mott)

36. This is an old Great Eastern coach, grounded at Ely and pictured in 1969. Though it has since been removed, it was a six-wheeled brake-van dating from 1891, of a type used on the Harwich - North of England Continental boat trains. The girder bridge carrying the main line across the River Ouse can be glimpsed in the background. (A.Mott)

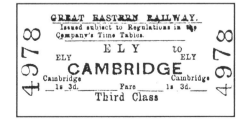

38. A view on 24 July 1988 which looks south from the end of the down platform, as a train leaves for Cambridge. Note that the centre-road has now gone, along with the corresponding signal-arm on the taller post of the bracket signal in the middle distance. (A Mott)

39. One way of avoiding waiting at the numerous level crossings at busy places on Fenland roads is to arrange a low (sometimes very low) bridge nearby to accommodate cars. Lorries, buses and high loads have no alternative but to wait at the gates, left. (A.Mott)

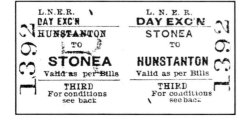

40. A Sprinter runs south across the A142 Newmarket road in November 1991. Ely Cathedral with its unusual octagonal lantern tower attracts visitors, many travelling by rail. Full lifting barriers were installed early in 1990. (A.Mott)

41. A southward view, from the north end of the Ely's down platform on 22nd January 1992 shows colour light signals ready to displace the semaphores on 11th May of that year. A large group waits on the island platform, detrained no doubt from the standing Sprinter, while the down platform road displays some very dubious trackwork. (A.Mott)

42. This view southwards from the north end of Ely station on 12th May 1992 shows that the work of electrifying the Cambridge/King's Lynn line is under way. The down line has been completely dug out and the platform itself was to be refaced. The disruption to services to and from Ely was, naturally, comprehensive, the station being completely closed for some months. Electric services started on 24th August 1992. (A.Mott)

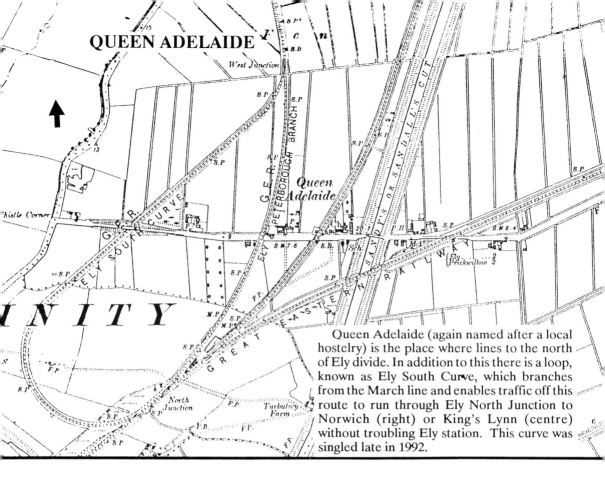

QUEEN ADELAIDE

Queen Adelaide (again named after a local hostelry) is the place where lines to the north of Ely divide. In addition to this there is a loop, known as Ely South Curve, which branches from the March line and enables traffic off this route to run through Ely North Junction to Norwich (right) or King's Lynn (centre) without troubling Ely station. This curve was singled late in 1992.

An immense distribution centre has been established east of North Junction. G.G. Papworth trades as part of the Potter Group Ltd and as such commenced rail operations at Queen Adelaide in 1981. By 1992, the goods received in by rail included the following:

Dedicated stone trains unloaded through a computerised bulk discharge system - Approximately 100,000 tonnes per annum, origination at UK quarry sites.

Powder products for the pharmaceutical industry - Approximately 5,000 tonnes per annum, originating in France.

Tinned fruit and juices - Approximately 10,000 tonnes per annum originating in Italy.

High quality paper on reels - Approximately 10,000 tonnes per annum, originating in Austria.

Engine components - Approximately 2,000 tonnes per annum originating in Germany.

Miscellaneous goods (household, timber etc.) - Approximately 10,000 Tonnes per annum. Various sources.

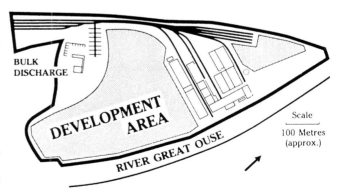

The traffic was handled by the firm's own locomotives, an ex-BR class 08 no. 08202 and a Thomas Hill Sentinel 0-6-0 DH (150C of 1965).

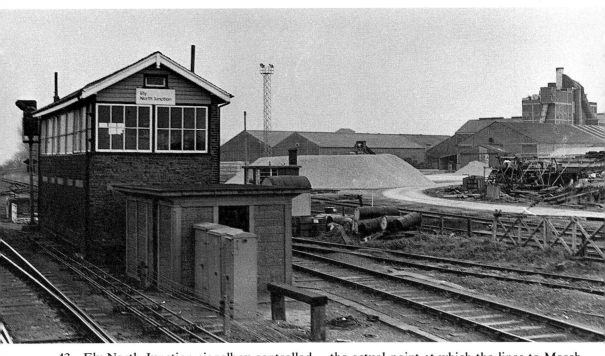

43. Ely North Junction signalbox controlled this traffic until the re-signalling of the area was completed on 11th May 1992. It stood a little to the south of Queen Adelaide, marking the actual point at which the lines to March, King's Lynn and Norwich diverge. This view looks north on 4th April 1988. (A.Mott)

From top to bottom on the right are the routes to March, Kings Lynn and Norwich. The sidings on the outskirts of Ely are on the left.

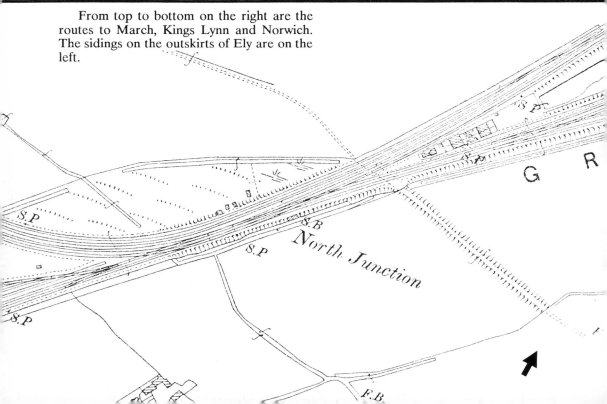

CHETTISHAM

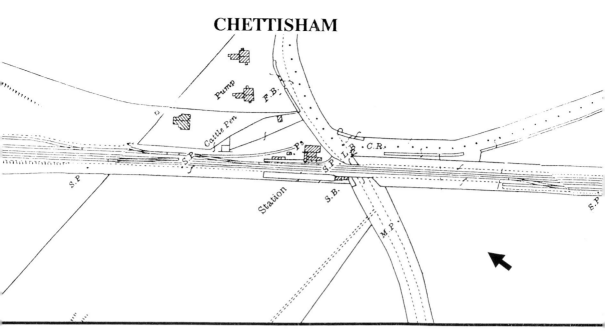

Chettisham village lies three miles north of Ely - the station was a little more by rail - and is not a large community. However, a station was established at the point where the railway crossed the A10 road and, later than this 1901 survey, a grain storage facility grew up in the southern angle between road and railway.

44. Chettisham (spelled Chittisham until 1st August 1901) was the first station out of Ely on the line towards March. This pre-WWII view looks towards Ely, on a summer afternoon with very little stirring. (D.Thompson)

45. Chettisham lost its passenger service on 13th June 1960, but got it back, temporarily, in 1991-92 during the electrification work at Ely, when makeshift, shelterless platforms were built on the site of the demolished originals, and a service of buses was provided for transit to connecting services. This picture, taken in October 1991, shows the Ely end of the temporary platform, with the signalbox (abolished from 9th May 1992), guarding the level crossing and seemingly little changed from 50 years earlier. (A.Mott)

46. This is Chettisham signalbox from the south, on 18th October 1991, with the station house derelict but still railway property. Note the survival of the northerly support of the old platform shelter seen in picture 44, though one doubts whether firebuckets still hang on the other side. Goods traffic ceased on 13th July 1964. (A.Mott)

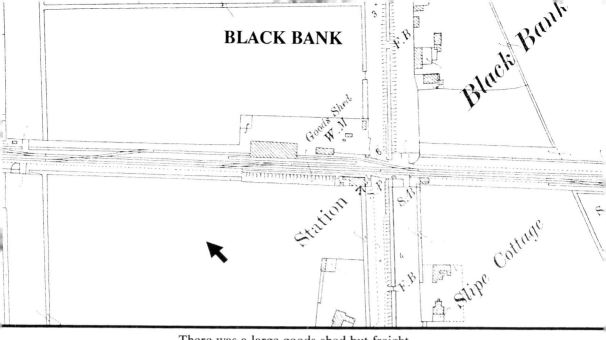

BLACK BANK

There was a large goods shed but freight
ceased on 19th April 1965. There are up and
down refuge sidings shown.

47. Black Bank station, seemingly in the
middle of nowhere, did in fact serve the nearby
village of Downham, which lies to the west of
the railway: indeed the station was called Little
Downham until November 1853, when it was
renamed, presumably to avoid confusion with
nearby Downham Market. This photograph
dates from the 1930s and looks south. The
signalbox is similar in pattern to that at
Chettisham, but is set on a timber base rather
than one of brick. The private owner wagons
on the left belong to Messrs Coote & Warren,
a Peterborough firm of coal merchants.
(D.Thompson)

48. This view is northwards during the 1950s as a class 31 diesel brings a parcels train through the station. The station building was of a prefabricated kind often found on Fenland railways, sometimes as here, weatherboarded, but occasionally more cheaply waterproofed with a layer of "tar paper". The tall lower-quadrant signal beside the station building, has now given way to a shorter, upper-quadrant type at the end of the platform.
(D.Thompson)

49. We look north from the signalbox in 1985, as a class 47 diesel brings the 1930 ex-Manchester (train 1E87) through the station towards Ely. Note that the siding to the goods shed has now gone, though the shed remains in commercial use. Goods service was withdrawn on 19th April 1965. (J.Ellis)

50. James Ellis was a signalman at Black Bank, and is here seen at work during 1985, with a train approaching from the south. The trackplan shows a very simple layout, and it is worth noting that the signalman's traditional stove has given way to electric kettle and hot-water heater. The station lost its passenger service on 17th June 1963. (J.Ellis)

51. On 21st January 1992, a stone aggregate train was derailed at Black Bank, damaging about two miles of track. Repairs were quickly under way, as this photograph, taken on the same day, shows. (A.Mott)

WELNEY WASH

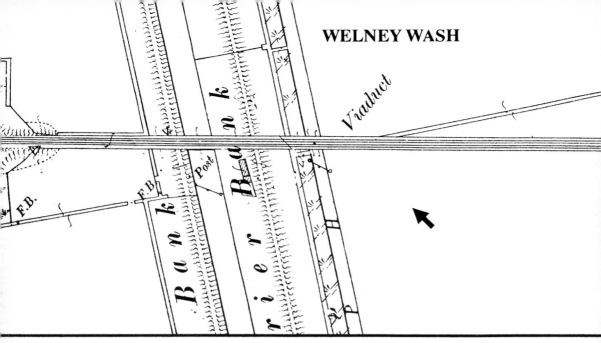

A narrow strip of land between the Old Bedford River or River Delph and the New Bedford River (Hundred Foot Drain) is used as a sort of safety valve in times of wet weather. Side-sluices in the rivers are opened, and excess water is allowed to flood the central area, thus easing pressure on the main waterways and, incidentally, providing a habitat for wintering wildfowl. The railway crosses this "Wash", mostly on embankment. The map shows the south end of the crossing.

52. This picture shows the construction of the lattice girder bridge across the New Bedford River, the southerly border of Welney Wash. As the main girder is eased sideways into position on a small-wheeled trolley, several workmen look on anxiously.
(March Museum)

MANEA

53. This early picture of Manea station looks towards Ely. Note once again that the signal is on what we would consider to be the wrong side, presumably for reasons of visibility. (March Museum,)

Manea - pronounced Maynee - also had a large goods shed for what was a small community, but agricultural products were of prime consideration here, far more so than were mere passengers. For all that, however, Manea is the only surviving intermediate station between March and Ely, though goods traffic was discontinued from 18th April 1966.

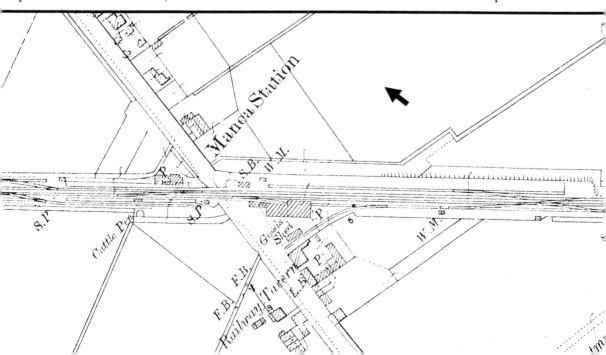

54. This is the same view, but 90 or so years on. Most buildings have gone, though the signalbox remains, as does the row of cottages on the right. A bus-stop type shelter is the only refuge on the new platform seen in November 1991. (A.Mott)

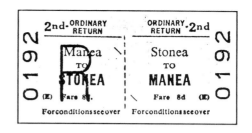

2nd. ORDINARY RETURN	ORDINARY RETURN 2nd
Manea TO STONEA	Stonea TO MANEA
(E) Fare 8.	Fare 8d (E)
For conditions see over	For conditions see over

0192   0192

55. We look now in the opposite direction as a Norwich-bound Sprinter runs past the station; it makes do with the original platform on that side. Note that the wooden fencing of the early picture has given way to post and rail, and lighting is no longer by oil. (A.Mott)

56. The signalbox is of a pattern now becoming familiar, though by November 1991 the steps and balcony have been replaced with slotted angle. A coal bucket stands thereon. By 1992, only two trains stopped each way, weekdays only. (A.Mott)

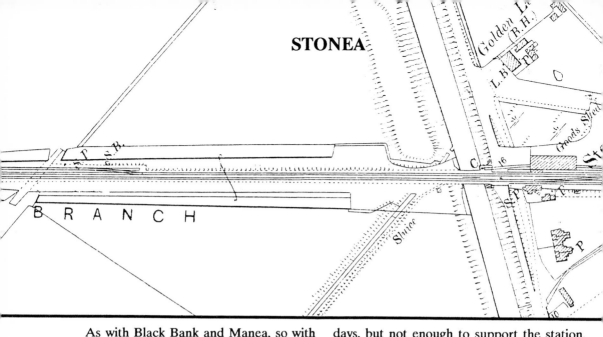

STONEA

As with Black Bank and Manea, so with Stonea (Stownee), an even smaller place than the last, built beside the Sixteen Foot River. At the time of this survey there seems to have been little there other than the station, a pub and a couple of cottages. There is a little more these days, but not enough to support the station, which closed for goods on 28th December 1964 and to passengers on 7th November 1966. There is a long headshunt on the right and a refuge siding on the left.

57. A Craven DMU crosses the Sixteen Foot River as it approaches Stonea from the north during the 1950s. There were more timber buildings here, but the station house lacks cross bracing on its weatherboards. (D.Thompson)

58. Beyond the station building lay the level crossing, this picture dated 1st June 1963 showing the north end of the platform. To the right of the level crossing the avoiding road passed beneath both the small timber building and the platform. (R.M.Casserley)

59. No. 158766 is approaching the decking of the avoiding bridge on 12th December 1991. Note the modern building which has replaced the timber hut seen earlier. The gates were still hand operated. (A.Mott)

3. St Ives towards March

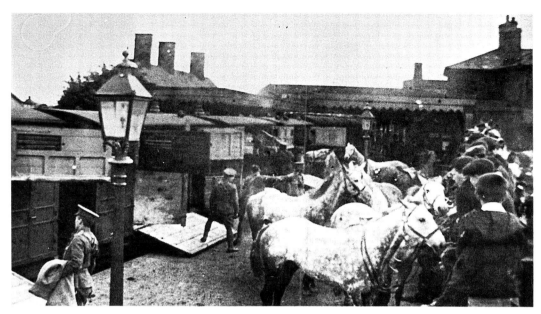

60. It is 1914, and the Fife and Forfar Yeomanry is entraining its transport for France in the station yard at St Ives, watched by what seems to be most of the juvenile population of the town. How many of these noble beasts returned, one wonders...? (R.Howse / Norris Museum, St Ives)

The station at St Ives was built in the angle formed by the junction of the lines to Huntingdon (left) and March (top), but most of the goods facilities lay to the March side of the complex. Beyond the large goods shed a branch led to the cattle market, an important part of St Ives life, and there was another branch to a mill a little further north. This section is now lost beneath a by-pass road. Lower right is the line from Cambridge.

61. St.Ives signalbox is seen in the 1930s. It stood on the platform, in the angle formed by the junction of the Huntingdon and March lines. This view is from the Cambridge platform on the March side, and the semaphore signal protects the junction from the Huntingdon direction.
(G.A.Shipp / Norris Museum, St Ives)

62. Class K1 2-6-0 no. 62040 of March shed (31B) engages in some shunting at St Ives on 28th August 1954. A varied assortment of wagons stands behind, and, presumably, the locomotive will shortly be doing something about the brakevan standing on the main line. (E.Sawford)

63. In sharp contrast to the previous view comes this scene of desolation in 1969. The branch left was to St. Ives Cattle Market and a coal drop, an unusual feature for the Fenland Railways. (A.Mott)

64. This shot, taken at the same time and place, looks back towards the station, which had lost its passenger service to March two years before, on 6th March 1967. Goods traffic ceased on 18th April 1966 with the exception of Aggregate traffic, which was shunted there until the station was demolished in about 1977. Passenger trains to Huntingdon had been withdrawn on 15th June 1959 but those to Cambridge continued until 5th October 1970. (A.Mott)

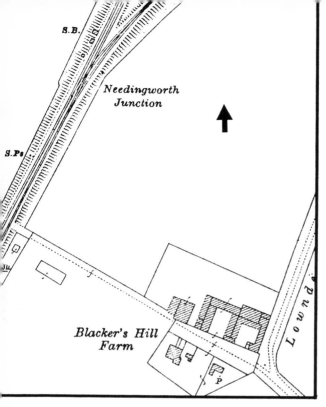

NEEDINGWORTH JUNCTION

Needingworth Junction was the point at which the branch from Ely via Sutton joined the St Ives/March route. It was never a very lucrative project. It opened on 10th May 1878 and closed to passengers on 2nd February 1931, but remained open to goods until 5th October 1964.

65. About one mile to the south of Needingworth Junction the line crossed the St Ives to Earith road (A1123) at a level crossing. When this picture was taken in the 1950s the crossing keeper still had duties to perform, though his cottage was beginning to look rather dilapidated. Again it is a standard fenland "prefab", this time with waterproof sheeting instead of weatherboards.
(B.Nunn / Mott Coll.)

SOMERSHAM

66. This is Somersham station as the prospective traveller would have seen it between the Wars. The now familiar avoiding road lies to the right of the level crossing and the elaborate four-way footbridge. In 1992 the level crossing was derelict and the bridge girders had been removed so that all traffic can use the road to the right.
(Huntingdon Record Office)

67. This northward view is from the 1950s. The signalbox, a largish one as befitted the goods facilities, stands beyond the down starting signal post. The box has been re-sited since the survey, when it was nearer to the end of the up (right-hand) platform.
(D.Thompson)

68. This is the view through the station towards St Ives on 1st June 1963. Gas lighting is still in use, and it is perhaps remarkable that the more solid building, brick as opposed to timber, is built on the east (left) side, the side furthest from the town, which had about 1400 inhabitants at this time. (R.M.Casserley)

69. The timber building was an attractive looking one however, less austere than the other, its hipped roof no doubt adding to this effect. This view, taken on 1st June 1963, looks north - Ramsey Junction is beyond the vans and the signalbox. (R.M.Casserley)

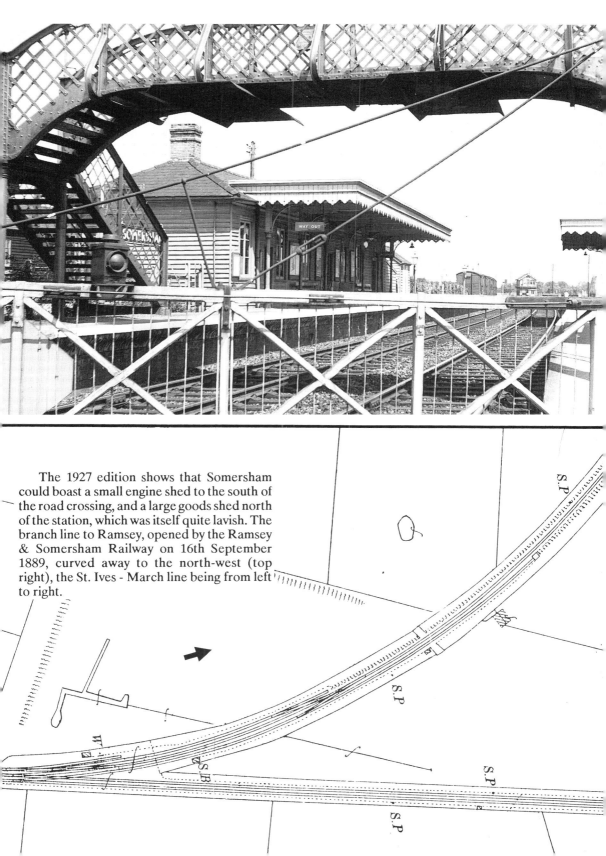

The 1927 edition shows that Somersham could boast a small engine shed to the south of the road crossing, and a large goods shed north of the station, which was itself quite lavish. The branch line to Ramsey, opened by the Ramsey & Somersham Railway on 16th September 1889, curved away to the north-west (top right), the St. Ives - March line being from left to right.

4. Ramsey East Branch
PIDLEY SIDING

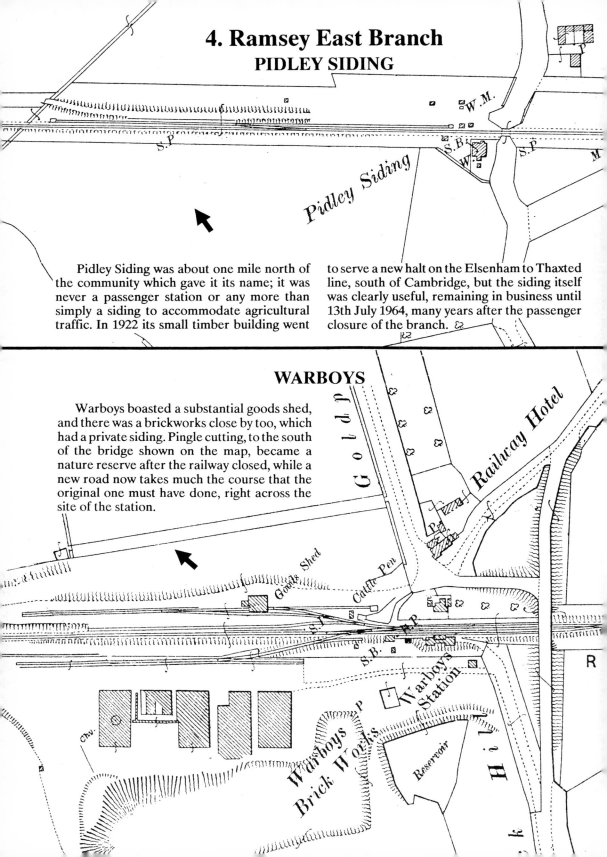

Pidley Siding was about one mile north of the community which gave it its name; it was never a passenger station or any more than simply a siding to accommodate agricultural traffic. In 1922 its small timber building went to serve a new halt on the Elsenham to Thaxted line, south of Cambridge, but the siding itself was clearly useful, remaining in business until 13th July 1964, many years after the passenger closure of the branch.

WARBOYS

Warboys boasted a substantial goods shed, and there was a brickworks close by too, which had a private siding. Pingle cutting, to the south of the bridge shown on the map, became a nature reserve after the railway closed, while a new road now takes much the course that the original one must have done, right across the site of the station.

70. Warboys was the only intermediate station between Somersham and Ramsey East. In this picture an Adams Class 61 0-4-4T shunts a short rake of wagons towards the goods shed. These engines were introduced in 1875, but with front cabs only - the weatherboard at the bunker end is a later addition to make the lives of the engine crew a little more comfortable. (Huntingdon Record Office)

71. This is the same site 60 years later, looking towards Ramsey along the deserted platforms. The branch lost its passenger service on 22nd September 1930, and it is remarkable that so much was visible, even after 40 years. The goods shed, on the right, is still in commercial use today, though a new road now cuts across the station site. (A.Mott)

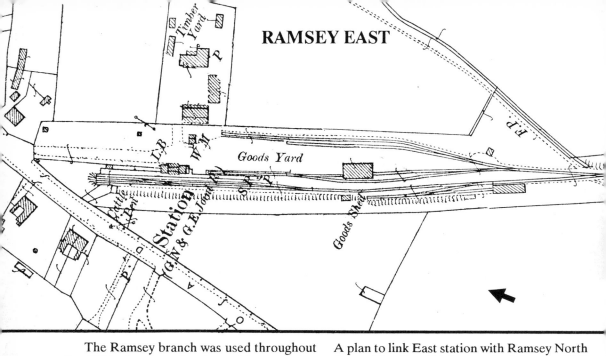

RAMSEY EAST

Timber Yard

Goods Yard

Goods Shed

Station (G.N. & G.E. Joint Rly.)

The Ramsey branch was used throughout the 1950s for occasional seaside excursion traffic to Clacton and other east coast resorts. The area to the south-east of Ramsey East station site is now a golf course, but would have been open country when the branch was built.

A plan to link East station with Ramsey North (owned by the GE but worked by the GN) failed for various reasons, though possibly the Somersham to Ramsey line might have survived a little longer if it had become a through route.

72. An F7 Class 2-4-2T stands at Ramsey East with a Somersham-bound train in early LNER days. The LMS cattle van in the siding is a visitor, a "long" type van built for the Midland Railway in 1921. The carriages are ex-Great Eastern 6-wheelers dating from about the turn of the century. The station was "Ramsey High Street" until 1st July 1923. (D.Thompson)

73. The RCTS made a tour of eastern branch lines on 24 July 1955, which included the Somersham to Ramsey East line. Here the train, hauled by Class J17 no.65562 pauses at Ramsey East before returning along the branch. Public freight services were withdrawn on 17th September 1956.
(A.E.Bennett)

February 1890

SOMERSHAM and RAMSEY.—Great Eastern.								
Liverpool Street,	mrn	mrn		mrn	aft	mrn	aft	aft	aft
LONDON 126 ....dep	6 0	7 22		9 10	....	1155	....	2 32	5 15
Somersham ....dep	9 17	1042		1144	1236	2 25	3 55	5 17	7 33
Warboys	9 27	1052		1151	1246	2 35	4 5	5 11	7 43
Ramsey (High St.) 167 a	9 33	1058		1157	1252	2 41	4 11	5 17	7 49
High Street,	mrn	mrn		mrn	aft	aft	aft	aft	aft
Ramsey ....dep	8 10	10 0		11 5	12 4	1 51	3 19	4 20	6 54
Warboys	8 16	10 6		1111	1210	1 57	3 25	4 26	7 0
Somersham 131 ....arr	8 26	1016		1121	1220	2 7	3 35	4 36	7 10
127 LONDON (L'pool St.) a	1110	....		....	2 52	....	6 8	8 30	....

July 1915

SOMERSHAM and RAMSEY.—Great Eastern.														
Miles.	Down.	Week Days only.					Miles.	Up.	Week Days only.					
	Liverpool Street,	mrn	mrn	non	aft		aft	aft	aft			High Street Station,	mrn	mrn	mrn		aft	aft	aft		aft	aft
	315 London ....dep	6 48	8 40	12 0			2 35	....	5 52				Ramsey............dep	7 38	10 0		1025		1 23	5	4*20		5 28	7 25
	315 " (St. Pancras)	....	....	103			....		3 35			2¼	Warboys............	7 44	10 6		1032		1 18	15	4 26		5 34	7 32
—	Somersham ....dep	9 14	1148	2 19	3 55		5 06	5 7	58			7	Somersham 315....arr	7 51	1016		1042		1 28	27	4 36		5 44	7 44
4¾	Warboys	3 8	9 26	1158	2 29	4 5		5 10	6 15	8		8¾	315 London (St. Pan.)arr					1 35						
7	Ramsey (High St.) * ..arr	9 32	12 4	2 35	4 11		5 16	6 21	8 14			83	315 " (L'poolSt.)	1019	2 7				2 7				8 20	
* About ¾ mile to Great Northern Station.															

July 1929

SOMERSHAM and RAMSEY (East).													
Miles.	Down.	Week Days only.					Miles.	Up.	Week Days only.				NOTES.
	Liverpool Street	mrn	mrn	mrn M		aft	aft		Ramsey (East) ....dep	mrn	mrn	mrn M D	aft	aft	aft M		A Arrives at 8 23 aft. on Tues., Weds., and Thurs.
	879 London ....dep	5 50	8 30	1150		2 34	....			7 36	10 0	1020	....	1 03	05 35		B About ¼ mile to Ramsey (North) Station.
—	Somersham ....dep	9 11	1182	19		5 46	10	2¾	Warboys............	7 42	1016	1026	....	1 68	75 41		D Except Mondays.
4¾	Warboys ......(below)	9 23	1198	2 29		5 14	22	7	Somersham 879...arr	7 52	1016	1036	....	1 16	3 19 5 51		M Mondays only.
7	Ramsey (East) B ...arr	9 30	1134	2 35		5 20	6 29	83	879 London (L. St.)arr	1023	2 7	2 7	....	5 9	6 10 8A23		

74. By 1957 decay had set in. This view, taken on 14th April, shows a rake of varied open wagons on weed-grown track, opposite a platform which is in little better shape. The population of the town was only a little over 5000 at this time. (H.C.Casserley)

75. No, this isn't the Warboys goods shed again, though it must be admitted that the similarity is striking. It is the site of Ramsey East station, as seen in February 1992. (A.Mott)

St. Ives towards March continued

CHATTERIS

76. Chatteris boasted an imposing station building situated on the town, or east, side of the line. The arched facade was unique on this line, and was repeated on the platform side of the building. (Chatteris Museum)

Chatteris station was built on the west side of the town it served, and received the goods facilities it no doubt felt to be its due. It was the main town between St Ives and March, but this did not, of course, prevent its station from dying when the rest of the railway did - it closed to passengers on 6th March 1967 and to goods just under a year earlier, on 18 April 1966.

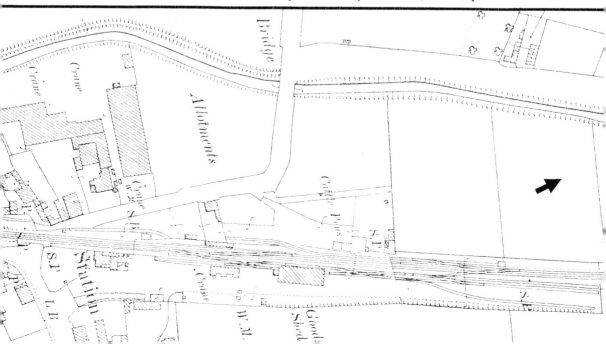

77. This westward view was taken from the high ground (over 25ft above sea level) on which a windmill was situated. It includes the signal box, a 10-ton capacity crane and Chatteris Enginering Works, which had sizable premises to the west of the line. The factory made machinery for gold and diamond mining. (Lens of Sutton)

78. This is the platform on the west side of the line; note the facing of engineering brick. It is not, perhaps, fanciful to suppose that the crowd on the platform is awaiting a train to March, having just finished work for the day at the nearby factory. (Lens of Sutton)

79. Chatteris signalbox must have been a moderately busy one - the trackplan is not complicated, but goods traffic would have prompted a fair number of shunting movements, even in the 1960s, the date of this picture. By this time the population was about 5500. (Chatteris Museum)

80. This view also dates from the 1960s, and looks north, towards March. Just what purpose was served by the small building at the far end of the main platform is not clear, but a substantial goods shed stands behind, and the signalbox is on the left. (Chatteris Museum)

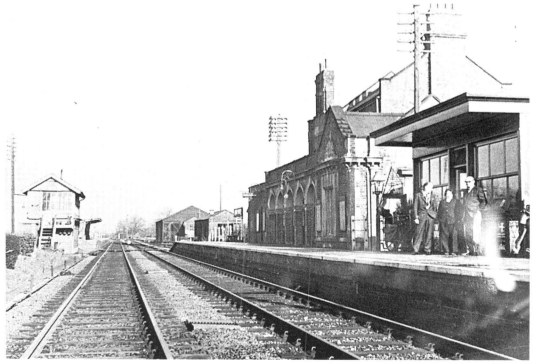

CHATTERIS DOCK

81. The bridge at Chatteris Dock was originally a timber structure and it was replaced with an iron girder construction in 1863. A girder can be seen slung on the crane in this picture of later repair work. The locomotive appears to be one of the class Y14 0-6-0s introduced by Worsdell in 1883, a specimen in the low-slung boiler series. (Chatteris Museum)

82. A sidelong view of the same construction train at Chatteris Dock, showing details of the bridge to better effect. Details of the cranes are not clear, but there seem to be no aids to lifting other than sheer muscle power. (Chatteris Museum)

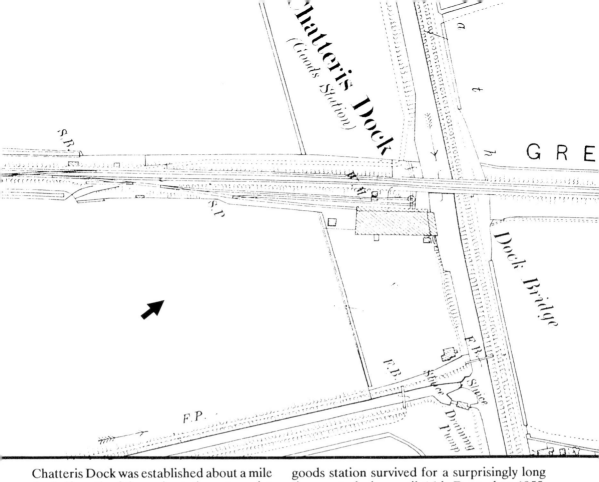

Chatteris Dock was established about a mile and a half north of the main station, at a point where the line crossed the Forty Foot Drain (or Vermuden's River named after the Dutchman who masterminded much of the drainage of the Fens in the 17th century). The goods station survived for a surprisingly long time, not closing until 16th December 1955, and it remained in use as a sack store until August 1957. Most traces have now disappeared beneath the new road which has taken over the course of the railway.

WIMBLINGTON

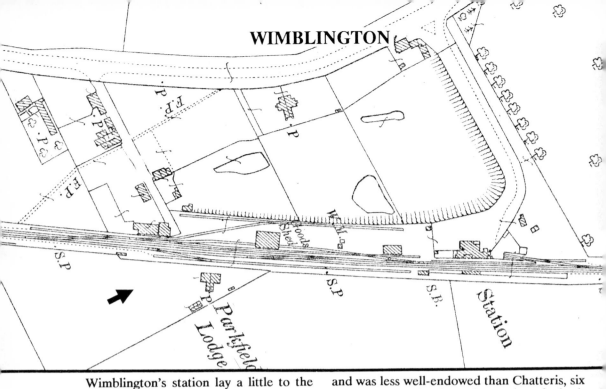

Wimblington's station lay a little to the south of the village, and perhaps it was hoped that it would thus gain business from nearby Doddington, though this never featured in its title. It lay on a cul-de-sac off the main road, and was less well-endowed than Chatteris, six miles to the south, whose closure dates for both goods and passengers it ultimately shared. Most remains have gone in deference to the new road, but the site can still be located.

83. A smart looking class B1 4-6-0 no.61301 pulls away southwards from Wimblington in 1958 with an up train to Cambridge. The signalbox can be seen just behind, and its presence would seem to be the reason for the very high signal post. (S.R.Payne)

84. The station at Wimblington had its main buildings on the west side of the line. By the time of this picture, which looks north on 3rd September 1956, the goods dock at the north end of the station had gone. (R.M.Casserley)

85. A freight train ambles southwards towards Wimblington headed by a class J17 0-6-0. In this view, taken from the spire of Wimblington church, a tar-papered crossing cottage can be seen beyond the train, guarding the level crossing at Eastwood End. (C.Parkinson)

86. Here, where trains once ran... This photograph, taken in March 1992, looks north from near the site of Wimblington station - the course of the line is now the A141 road from a point north of Wimblington to the roundabout south of Chatteris. (A.Mott)

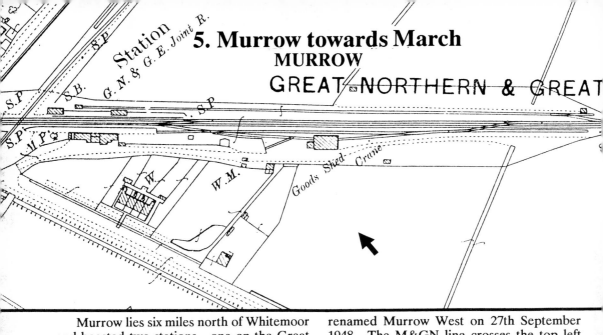

MURROW

GREAT NORTHERN & GREAT

Murrow lies six miles north of Whitemoor and boasted two stations - one on the Great Northern & Great Eastern Joint line, and Murrow East, which served the Midland & Great Northern Joint. The GN/GE station was renamed Murrow West on 27th September 1948. The M&GN line crosses the top left corner of the map. The crane was of 5-ton capacity.

87. Level crossing of two main lines is rare in this country - one still survives at Newark. The unthinkable happened at Murrow on 26th November 1925 when a M&GN train ran into one on the "Joint" line, frost having jammed the signal. The March 20-ton crane was one of two unique machines built at Stratford in use on the recovery work. A collision between two freight trains on the crossing on 4th November 1941 resulted in the destruction of the signalbox. A temporary box was in use until 1949. The flat-roofed replacement controlled colour light signals. (R.H.R.Garraway)

88. Ex-Great Central Railway Robinson 4-4-2 (LNER class C4) no.5192 pulls away from a station stop at Murrow with a northbound stopping train. By Nationalisation there were 20 of these engines left, numbered in the 2900 series. Note the GN somersault signal. (N.Rand Coll.)

89. This view looks south again, on 29th September 1967. The M&GN crossing has gone, and so have station and signalbox. Passenger traffic ceased on 6th July 1953, and goods six years before, on 1st September 1947. The goods shed survives on the right of the line, and a new signalbox has been built north of the site of the crossing. The link between the March line and what remains of the M&GN, can be seen curving away beyond the signalbox. This curve was brought into use on 2nd January 1961, enabling freight services to be maintained eastwards to Wisbech North and westwards to the brickworks at Dogsthorpe Siding. These were withdrawn in 1965 and 1966 respectively. (H.C.Casserley)

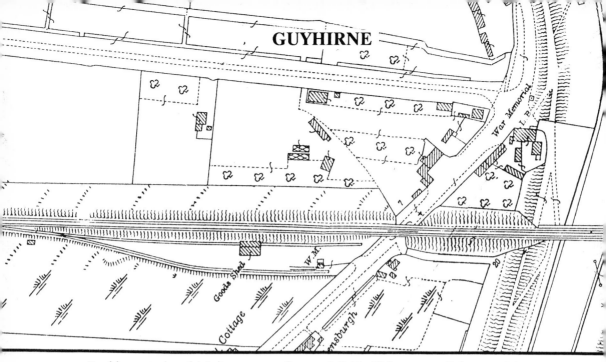

GUYHIRNE

Guyhirne station (right) was actually at Ring's End, some little way from its village, and closed to passengers on 5th October 1953. It was another instance where the railway persisted in contradicting the Ordnance Survey name of the village, usually using a final "e". Facilities were slight, restricted to some extent by the site, but there was a siding and goods shed (closed on 5th October 1964) to the north of the A47 Peterborough to Wisbech road (left).

90. This view of Guyhirne station, dating from around 1931, looks north - the station itself being on the left, beyond the signalbox. The girders span the Wisbech to March road at the north-eastern end of a short viaduct which survived intact until very recently. March lies three miles away to the right.
(H.Coates / Wisbech & Fenland Museum)

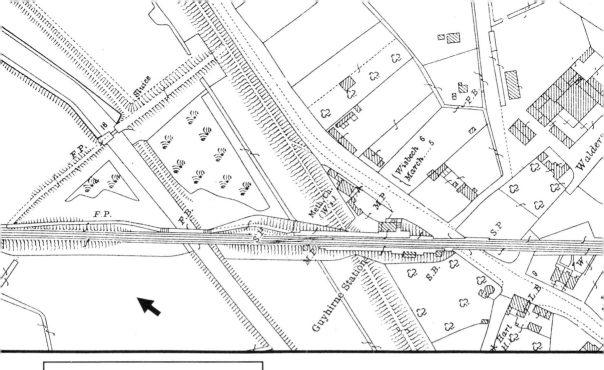

91. This view is taken from the south end of the station, looking north towards Murrow, the viaduct seen in the previous shot now being behind the camera. Facilities were not extensive, and the timber platform leaves something to be desired in the matter of levels. (D.Thompson)

WHITEMOOR YARD

The 1927 survey shows Grassmoor Junction at the north end of the complex. Whitemoor Yard was the first mechanised humpyard in Britain, and covered 68 acres at its largest, with about 50 miles of track. The up yard opened in March 1929, the down yard in 1931. Grassmoor Junction (top) commanded the northern end of the marshalling yard until 1929, when Twenty Foot River signalbox took over the control of the exit from the down yard and entry to the up yard. When the Joint Agreement was made it was settled that the line from Grassmoor Junction to March Loop Junction (at the south end of the Whitemoor complex) should be owned solely by the GER, with the GNR exercising running powers. The plan on the right shows the yard after complete development.

92. The additional locomotive shed is seen under construction on 26th April 1932, it becoming known as "Washout Shed" - see diagram. In 1952, March was the fourth largest depot in the Eastern Motive Power Area of the Eastern Region with an allocation of 165 engines. At that time Ely had five and Wisbech six. (R.H.R.Garraway)

93. This aerial view looks north and covers the entire expanse of Whitemoor's enormous complex. There are two engine sheds, both on the left, with the original Norwood yard, with its goods shed, in the centre of the picture. This yard was used to make up full loads of "smalls" traffic and minimise wagon movements. The main line curves past it on the right, and then straight as a die across the fen towards Guyhirne. The up hump yard lies on the right, with the down yard in the left distance. (March Museum)

94. Whitemoor Junction Box controlled the northern apex of the triangle with traffic to and from Peterborough, March, Wisbech and Murrow, as well as the traffic into the down and out of the up marshalling yards. (March Museum)

Connections in the March district in 1930, prior to the construction of Whitemoor Down Yard. (Railway Gazette)

96. The War is over, but this Riddles designed 2-10-0 still bears its WD emblem on the tender. No.73787 stands near the coaling tower at Whitemoor, on 6th April 1946. Many ex-WD 2-8-0s entered the stock of the LNER but no engines of this wheel arrangement. (H.C.Casserley)

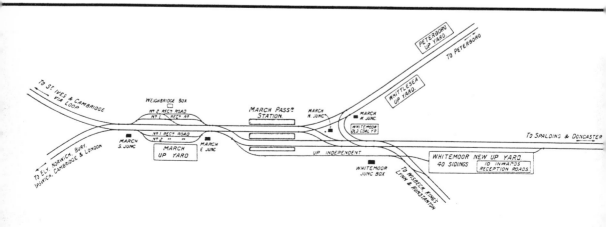

95. Ladies took on the jobs of platelayers during World War II. This gang is posed in front of the engine shed at the south end of the down reception sidings. (March Museum)

97. Shunting was the main business of Whitemoor, and on the same date an early diesel shunter pushes a rake of wagons over the hump in the down yard. A loaded van rolls away towards the sorting sidings, and as the locomotive continues to propel the train at a steady 2 mph so the subsequent "cuts" will fall away similarly. (H.C.Casserley)

98. Access to the sorting sidings was governed by the control towers, one on the up and another on the down side. This is a northward view from the up tower, with the main line beyond the trees. On the left is the gently graded train engine release line. Only the yard shunting engines were allowed on the steep part of the hump. The outer wheels of main line engines would have lost contact with the rails. (R.H.R.Garraway)

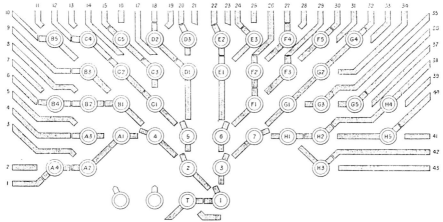

The control board consisted of a series of switches which controlled the points of the 43 sidings. A shunter walked the length of incoming train and wrote a "cut-card" showing the destination of each wagon or group of wagons. This card was conveyed by pneumatic tube to the control tower where the operator would set the switches which recorded the sequence of point movements on a set of seven pairs of rotating collector drums fitted with electromagnetic levers. These operated like pegs in a musical box and impinged on cams and switches to move the electric points.

Track circuits monitored the locations of rolling wagons. The "collector drums" acted as a memory for up to 50 "cuts" and a train of 70 wagons to be forwarded to up to 50 different destinations could be handled in a mere seven minutes. The board was similar to the panel of a modern signal box, push button switches activating electric point motors. Only nos. 1-7 could be worked automatically as described. "T" controlled the train engine release points, 1 was for the "king" points, 2 and 3 for the "queen" points and 4 to 7 for the "jacks". (Railway Gazette)

99. The speed of the wagons off the down hump was controlled by electromagnetic retarders, and it required a nice judgement to balance the weight of a particular wagon with the distance it had to travel, so that it had exactly the right momentum to reach the point

where it was wanted. The wagon in this 9th August 1960 view has just passed the "king" points, the first in the sequence on its way to its allotted siding, and will reach the "queen" points soon after it runs off the retarder. (C.V.Awdry)

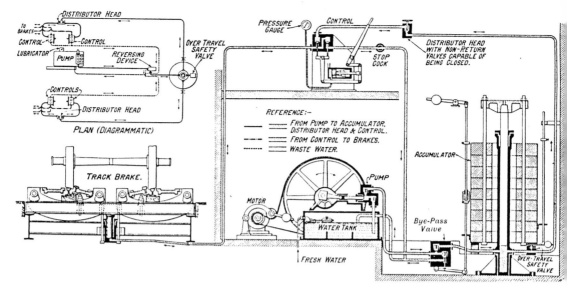

PLAN (DIAGRAMMATIC)

TRACK BRAKE.

REFERENCE:—
——— FROM PUMP TO ACCUMULATOR.
——— DISTRIBUTOR HEAD & CONTROL.
— — FROM CONTROL TO BRAKES.
······· WASTE WATER.

The LNER built its own direct current power station to provide electricity for the electromagnetic wagon retarders in the down yard and the motors for the hydraulic pumps of the up yard. Water was pressed to 1400 psi to work the wagon brakes which were designed by the German Dr Frolich. DC was also used for the point motors (110v), collector drums (36v), track circuit (12v) and yard lighting. (Railway Gazette)

100. This view looks north at Whitemoor Junction, where the former GN/GE line (left) joined the Wisbech branch, which can be seen curving away to the right, beyond the signalbox. On 25th March 1961 a stopping train, hauled by class 5 4-6-0 no.73001, comes off the "Joint" line and heads towards March station. (A.Curtis)

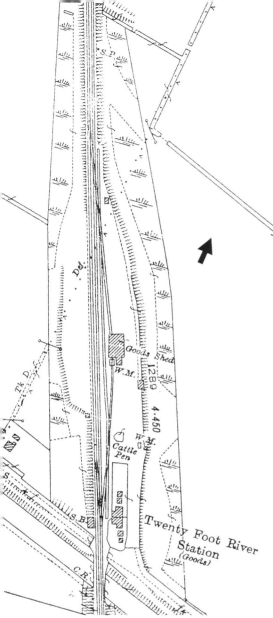

Public goods facilities were available just north of Whitemoor Yard until 13th July 1964.

101. By 10th May 1986, when the Railway & Canal Historical Society toured Whitemoor, activity was beginning to run down. By then it occupied only the southern half of the up yard, which was worked as a flat yard. Contrary to popular belief, not everything at Whitemoor was built to the standard gauge. This engineer's line was 2ft 6in gauge and was laid alongside the crippled-wagon siding, to move a manually propelled tool truck to where repairs were needed. (A.Mott)

102. The upper floor once contained the switch table, retarder controls and pneumatic tube receiver. The collector drum frame was located on the middle floor. Among the final items to stand was the up yard control tower, seen here during 1987. Whitemoor Prison, opened by Mrs. Norma Major in September 1991, now occupies the site. (A.Mott)

103. Wisbech had a royal visit on Saturday 18th April 1863, when the Prince and Princess of Wales were persuaded by the then Mayor of the town to break their journey back to London after honeymooning at Sandringham. It seems doubtful whether the happy couple are in this picture, the earliest known railway photograph taken at Wisbech. The locomotive is probably Sinclair 2-2-2 No.31.
(G.Gardiner / Wisbech Museum)

The sharp curve to the west of Wisbech station resulted from two companies reaching there from different directions. (See Historical Background - first paragraph) Wisbech Goods was consequently some little way from the passenger station, on a site of its own, and by 1992 was the location of the only railway activity surviving in the town. The site of the passenger station is now occupied by an old people's home. The scale is 15" to 1 mile.

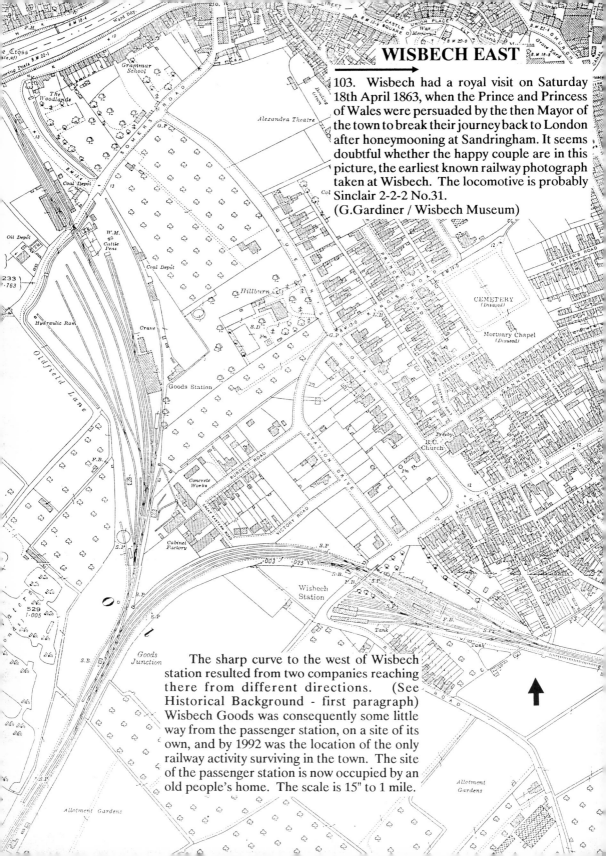

6. Wisbech towards March

104. This is the loop platform, looking west in about 1920. A Class Y6 0-4-0 "tram" engine waits at the platform to leave with a passenger train for Upwell, while the station staff pose nearby. Note what appears to be a portable weighing trolley to the right of the locomotive (A.Ingram Coll.)

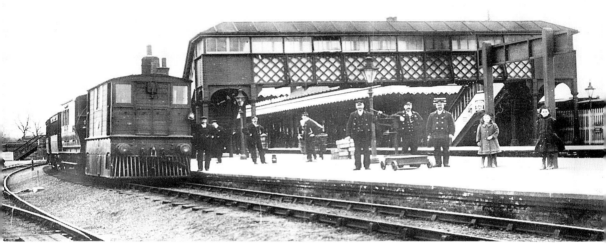

105. The track on the left of the previous picture led to the engine shed, seen here during the early 1960s when the town was occupied by about 17,500 souls. By then the two sheds had been reduced to one, and the steam "trams" had given way to diesel power. Very wisely, some engines were kept on standby at March shed during the diesels' first few months; they were needed more than once! (J.Stafford-Baker / A.Ingram)

106. Another shot from the early 1960s, this time looking west along the up platform. The footbridge just visible behind the train in picture 104 has now gone, and the GER signalbox (in which, so legend relates, band rehearsals were sometimes held) can be clearly seen. Wisbech's goods yard lies beyond the distant row of houses.
(J.Stafford-Baker / A.Ingram)

107. Brush D/E2 no.D5633 waits at Wisbech East with a short up passenger train to March in 1967. The tramway to Upwell had closed the previous year although it had not carried passengers since 1928. Note that already the "tram" platform, on the right, is becoming unkempt, and there are weeds elsewhere, too.
(A.Ingram)

108. The Wisbech and March Railway Action Committee ran an inaugural excursion to Cambridge on Saturday 23rd September 1978. The train is seen awaiting departure from the loading dock at Wisbech East Goods. Hopes for a re-opening of the line for a passenger service now appear to have been dashed by BR. While track remains however there is always the possibility of revival if the local authorities are prepared to assist. (A.Ingram)

109. The freight service was still operating in 1992. This view, dated 24th October 1988, depicts the loading of produce from Spiller's cannery into long-bodied wagons. Traffic from the nearby Metal Box factory was also handled here. (A.Mott)

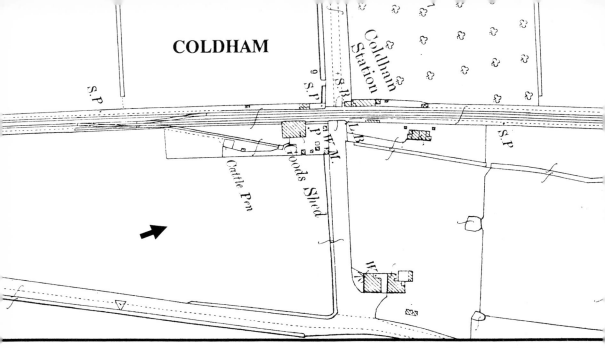

COLDHAM

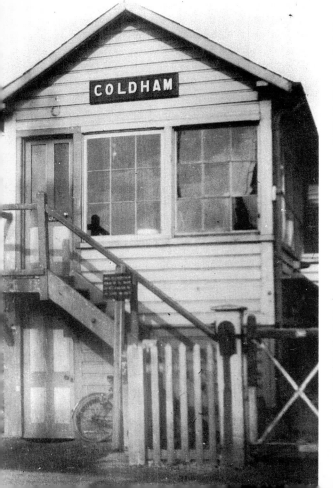

About three miles south of Wisbech the line was crossed by a minor road at Waldersea Drove Siding, never more than a freight facility. Coldham, another mile and a half further south, was slightly endowed also - there was a small yard and goods shed south of the level crossing, while the station lay to the north of it. Coldham - at first called Pear Tree Hill, but renamed on 1st September 1876 - closed for passengers on 7th March 1966, and for goods on 19th April 1965. Waldersea Drove had succumbed on 13th July 1964.

110. Very little ever seemed to happen at Coldham, the most notable feature that the writer (CA) recalls being the plaster(?) "cold ham" which lay beneath each station name-board. This shot of the small, weather-boarded signalbox dates from 1947. Behind the box stood one of the familiar pre-fab houses, boarded with cross-bracing. Nothing remained in 1992, other than the level crossing and its gates, which were crew operated. (N.Rand)

7. March
MARCH

111. The station facade dates from 1885, and this early view is taken from a postcard. Not a scene bustling with activity, but this belies the general, for things could, and did, become extremely busy. March is the principal town in the Isle of Ely and by the 1960s had grown to house over 13,000 folk.
(March Museum)

112. Much railway shunting and goods delivery and collection used to be done by horses, and at a place such as March the equine strength was an essential part of the staff. Here the handlers, and others, pose for the camera in the late 1920s. (March Museum)

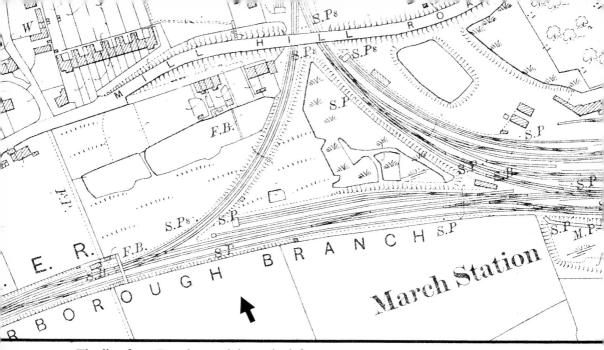

The line from Peterborough is on the left with that from Ely on the right. Beyond the top of the triangle is Whitemoor Box and the junction for Wisbech and the Murrow - Spalding line. March Yard is on the right. The main part of the town lies some half-mile south of the station.

113. There were even visits to March by famous old engines. Stirling 8ft Single No.1 calls, with a special train in the Cambridge direction, in 1938.
(M.B.Evans / March Museum)

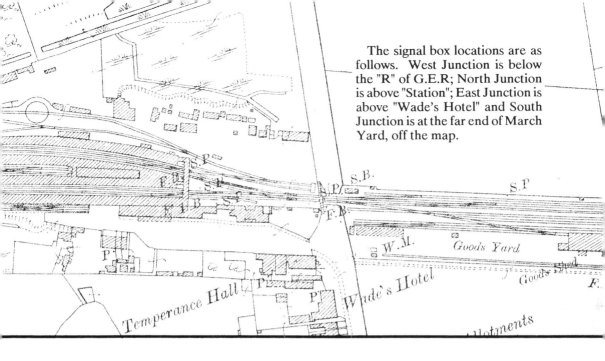

The signal box locations are as follows. West Junction is below the "R" of G.E.R; North Junction is above "Station"; East Junction is above "Wade's Hotel" and South Junction is at the far end of March Yard, off the map.

114. This view, taken on 3rd April 1956, shows the 10.15am ex-Cambridge to King's Lynn stopping train approaching March from the south. Once halted at the station it will be routed via the Wisbech East line. The engine is class D16/3 4-4-0 no.62562, and the stock is very mixed, a Thompson suburban centre-lavatory car leading. (P.Hay)

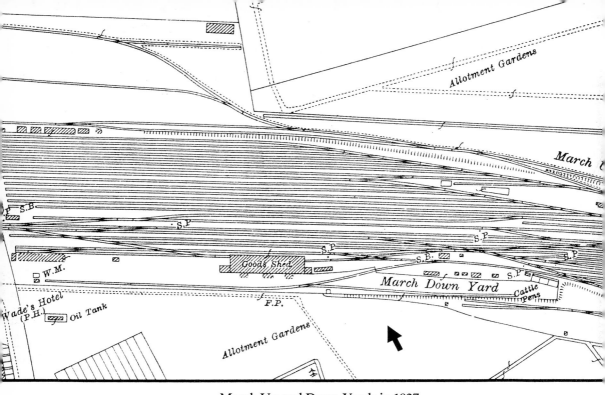

March Up and Down Yards in 1927.

115. During the spring of 1956 a grubby class J17 0-6-0 no.65577 comes over the level crossing east of March station and approaches platform 3, bound for Whitemoor. The lower quadrant signal on the right relates to the up main line, enabling southbound trains to start from this down platform. The buildings on the right are those of the original Eastern Counties Railway station, now demolished - see picture 120. (P Hay)

116. This view looks west towards the station from the level crossing, again on 3rd April 1956, as class D16/3 4-4-0 no.62605 comes off the avoiding line. Class J69 0-6-0T no.68603 was the station pilot at this time. (P.Hay)

117. This view is west, taken during the early 1960s, and it includes the rather unattractive North signalbox. The station has a bay on the extreme left, and also on the right, the latter used by Wisbech line trains. The Peterborough line curves to the left of the signalbox, while the other leads to Whitemoor Junction. An east-north link formed the third side of the triangle, and lay beyond the shrubbery behind the signalbox. (A.Ingram)

118. We are looking in the same direction but now from the station footbridge, as a DMU from Peterborough draws to a halt at the platform in May 1986. The signal box has gone but March East Junction and South Junction boxes were still in use six years later. (A.Mott)

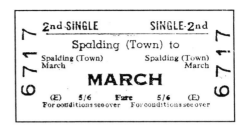

006

No exit   DO NOT CROSS

March

119. This photograph was taken on 15th January 1989 from the same spot as picture no. 116, pointing a contrast to what has happened to this station during the intervening 33 years. The avoiding line has become an engineers' siding. Platform 4 is devoid of track but platform 3 has a line to Whitemoor Junction for locomotive movements to the nearby depot and for freight services from Wisbech. (A.Mott)

120. Finally another view east, as diesel no.60006, heading a long rake of empties for the Peterborough line, enters the station for a crew change on 26th March 1991. The seven-siding yard to the left of the signalbox then handled all the freight traffic at March and that on the right housed the wagon repair facility of Marcroft Engineering. The population of the town grew with the development of the railway, whose influence seems in decline at present; only the future will tell whether the great days are really over. (A.Mott)

MP Middleton Press

Easebourne Lane, Midhurst, West Sussex. GU29 9AZ Tel: 01730 813169 Fax: 01730 812601
If books are not available from your local transport stockist, order direct with cheque, Visa or Mastercard, post free UK.

BRANCH LINES
Branch Line to Allhallows
Branch Lines to Alton
Branch Lines around Ascot
Branch Line to Ashburton
Branch Lines around Bodmin
Branch Line to Bude
Branch Lines around Canterbury
Branch Line to Cheddar
Branch Lines around Cromer
Branch Lines to East Grinstead
Branch Lines to Effingham Junction
Branch Line to Fairford
Branch Line to Hawkhurst
Branch Line to Hayling
Branch Lines to Horsham
Branch Line to Ilfracombe
Branch Line to Kingswear
Branch Lines to Launceston & Princetown
Branch Lines to Longmoor
Branch Line to Looe
Branch Line to Lyme Regis
Branch Lines around March
Branch Lines around Midhurst
Branch Line to Minehead
Branch Lines to Newport (IOW)
Branch Line to Padstow
Branch Lines around Plymouth
Branch Line to Selsey
Branch Lines around Sheerness
Branch Line to Tenterden
Branch Lines to Torrington
Branch Lines to Tunbridge Wells
Branch Line to Upwell
Branch Lines around Weymouth
Branch Lines around Wimborne
Branch Lines around Wisbech

NARROW GAUGE BRANCH LINES
Branch Line to Lynton
Branch Lines around Portmadoc 1923-46
Branch Lines around Porthmadog 1954-94
Branch Line to Southwold
Two-Foot Gauge Survivors

SOUTH COAST RAILWAYS
Ashford to Dover
Brighton to Eastbourne
Chichester to Portsmouth
Dover to Ramsgate
Hastings to Ashford
Portsmouth to Southampton
Ryde to Ventnor
Southampton to Bournemouth
Worthing to Chichester

SOUTHERN MAIN LINES
Bromley South to Rochester
Charing Cross to Orpington
Crawley to Littlehampton
Dartford to Sittingbourne
East Croydon to Three Bridges
Epsom to Horsham
Exeter to Barnstaple
Exeter to Tavistock
Faversham to Dover
Haywards Heath to Seaford
London Bridge to East Croydon
Orpington to Tonbridge
Swanley to Ashford
Tavistock to Plymouth
Victoria to East Croydon
Waterloo to Windsor

Waterloo to Woking
Woking to Portsmouth
Woking to Southampton
Yeovil to Exeter

EASTERN MAIN LINES
Fenchurch Street to Barking

COUNTRY RAILWAY ROUTES
Andover to Southampton
Bournemouth to Evercreech Jn.
Burnham to Evercreech Junction
Croydon to East Grinstead
Didcot to Winchester
Fareham to Salisbury
Frome to Bristol
Guildford to Redhill
Porthmadog to Blaenau
Reading to Basingstoke
Reading to Guildford
Redhill to Ashford
Salisbury to Westbury
Stratford Upon Avon to Cheltenham
Strood to Paddock Wood
Taunton to Barnstaple
Wenford Bridge to Fowey
Westbury to Bath
Woking to Alton
Yeovil to Dorchester

GREAT RAILWAY ERAS
Ashford from Steam to Eurostar
Clapham Junction 50 years of change
Festiniog in the Fifties
Festiniog in the Sixties
Isle of Wight Lines 50 years of change
Railways to Victory 1944-46

LONDON SUBURBAN RAILWAYS
Caterham and Tattenham Corner
Charing Cross to Dartford
Clapham Jn. to Beckenham Jn.
Crystal Palace and Catford Loop
East London Line
Finsbury Park to Alexandra Palace
Holborn Viaduct to Lewisham
Kingston and Hounslow Loops
Lewisham to Dartford
Lines around Wimbledon
London Bridge to Addiscombe
North London Line
South London Line
West Croydon to Epsom
West London Line
Willesden Junction to Richmond
Wimbledon to Epsom

STEAM PHOTOGRAPHERS
O.J.Morris's Southern Railways 1919-59

STEAMING THROUGH
Steaming through Cornwall
Steaming through East Sussex
Steaming through the Isle of Wight
Steaming through Kent
Steaming through West Hants
Steaming through West Sussex

TRAMWAY CLASSICS
Aldgate & Stepney Tramways
Barnet & Finchley Tramways
Bath Tramways
Bournemouth & Poole Tramways

Brighton's Tramways
Bristol's Tramways
Camberwell & W.Norwood Tramways
Clapham & Streatham Tramways
Dover's Tramways
East Ham & West Ham Tramways
Edgware and Willesden Tramways
Eltham & Woolwich Tramways
Embankment & Waterloo Tramways
Enfield & Wood Green Tramways
Exeter & Taunton Tramways
Gosport & Horndean Tramways
Greenwich & Dartford Tramways
Hampstead & Highgate Tramways
Hastings Tramways
Holborn & Finsbury Tramways
Ilford & Barking Tramways
Kingston & Wimbledon Tramways
Lewisham & Catford Tramways
Liverpool Tramways 1. Eastern Routes
Liverpool Tramways 2. Southern Routes
Maidstone & Chatham Tramways
North Kent Tramways
Portsmouth's Tramways
Reading Tramways
Seaton & Eastbourne Tramways
Southampton Tramways
Southend-on-sea Tramways
Southwark & Deptford Tramways
Stamford Hill Tramways
Thanet's Tramways
Victoria & Lambeth Tramways
Waltham Cross & Edmonton Tramways
Walthamstow & Leyton Tramways
Wandsworth & Battersea Tramways

TROLLEYBUS CLASSICS
Croydon Trolleybuses
Bournemouth Trolleybuses
Maidstone Trolleybuses
Reading Trolleybuses
Woolwich & Dartford Trolleybuses

WATERWAY ALBUMS
Kent and East Sussex Waterways
London's Lost Route to the Sea
London to Portsmouth Waterway
Surrey Waterways
West Sussex Waterways

MILITARY BOOKS and VIDEO
Battle over Portsmouth
Battle over Sussex 1940
Blitz over Sussex 1941-42
Bombers over Sussex 1943-45
Bognor at War
Military Defence of West Sussex
Secret Sussex Resistance
Sussex Home Guard
War on the Line
War on the Line VIDEO

OTHER BOOKS and VIDEO
Betwixt Petersfield & Midhurst
Brickmaking in Sussex
Changing Midhurst
Garraway Father & Son
Index to all Stations
South Eastern & Chatham Railways
London Chatham & Dover Railway

COLLECTORS GUIDES
Action Man 1966-69